The Biggest Carrot in the World

Written by
Cath Jones

Illustrated by
Jieting Chen

Poppy wanted to grow the biggest carrot in the world.

"Emma!" she said. "June is the perfect time for growing carrots! Let's enter a carrot growing contest! Then we could have a carrot feast too!"

The rabbits hoed and raked the ground. Then they scattered carrot seeds.

For weeks, they tended their carrot patch with care.

At last, the carrots were ready to harvest. One of the carrots was **HUGE!**

Poppy and Emma pulled up loads of carrots. But when they tried to pull up the biggest carrot, it wouldn't budge!

A mole was watching them.

"Wow!" said the mole. "That carrot is **HUGE!** If we can join your carrot feast, we will help you to dig it up. I will get my friends and we will help you in the morning."

But in the night, the carrot kept growing. It creaked as it grew bigger and bigger.

It grew down the rabbits' chimney.

The tip of the carrot burst into Poppy's bedroom. It woke Poppy up!

"Eek!" shrieked Poppy. "That carrot poked me. How rude!"

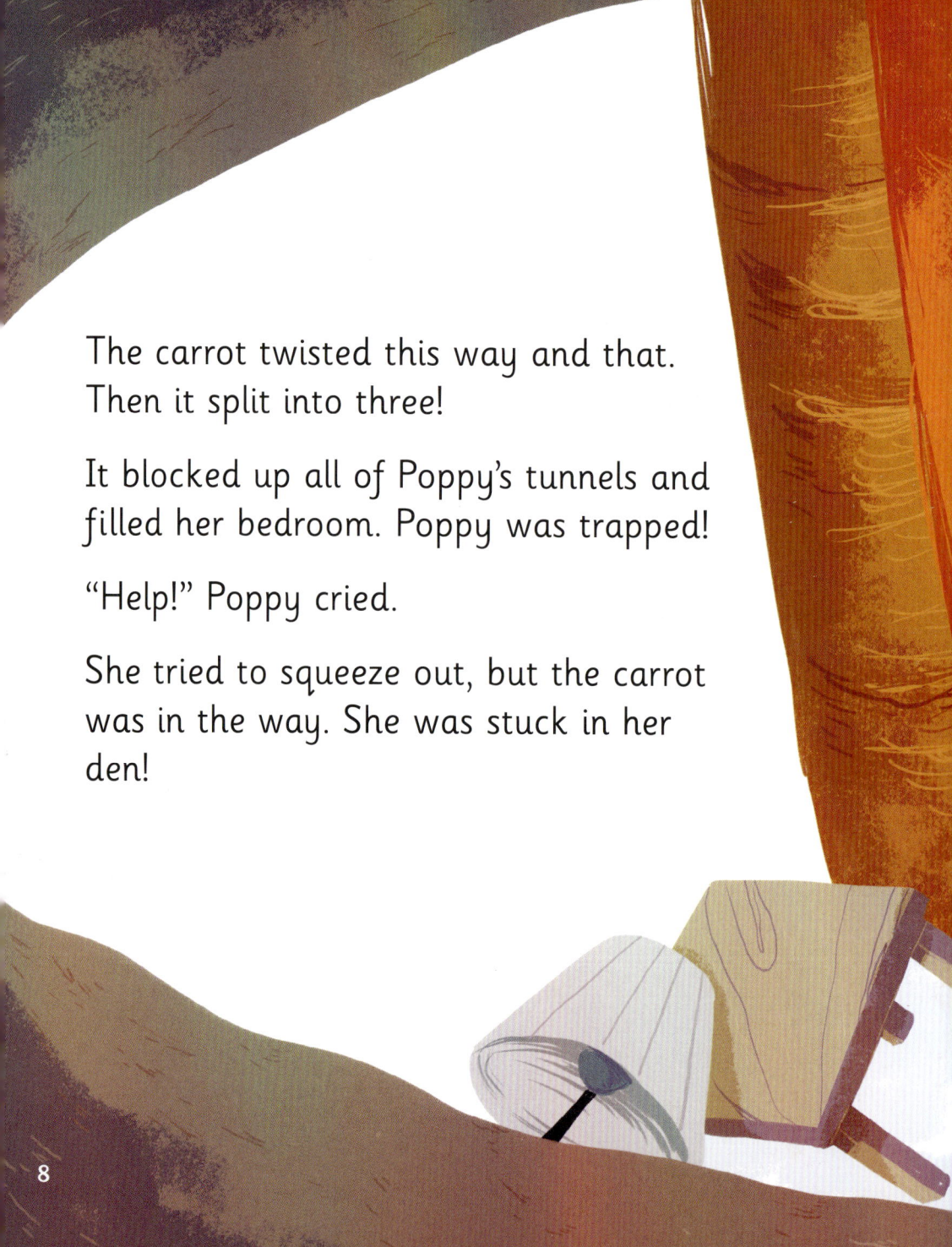

The carrot twisted this way and that. Then it split into three!

It blocked up all of Poppy's tunnels and filled her bedroom. Poppy was trapped!

"Help!" Poppy cried.

She tried to squeeze out, but the carrot was in the way. She was stuck in her den!

The moles set to work. They dug a tunnel and helped Poppy escape from the carrot.

But now Poppy had nowhere to sleep. Her bed was broken and her den was full of carrot.

Poppy tried sleeping outside, but her dreams were full of creepy carrots.

"The carrots are going to get me!" she shrieked.

"We need to get rid of that carrot!" Poppy cried.

"Let's use a pulley," Mole said.

All of the moles hung on to the rope.

"Pull!" yelled Poppy. Very slowly, the carrot slid out of the rabbits' den.

Emma took the carrot away on a big truck. She drove it to the carrot contest.

"Thank goodness," Poppy said. "Now we are safe from the creepy carrot!"

The next day, Poppy's telephone rang. It was the chief judge from the carrot contest.

"Your carrot is a champ. You're the winner of the carrot contest!" he said.

"We won!" laughed Poppy.

"Did we win lots of money?" Emma asked.

"No," said the judge, "but you win a very big cup!"

Poppy and Emma got their **HUGE** carrot back too.

The carrot and the cup were perfect for the rabbits' carrot feast.

Everybody had carrot soup!